Spell It

The pocket word book for schools

Gerald Solomons

M Macmillan Education

© Gerald Solomons 1980

All rights reserved. No part of this publication may be reproduced or transmitted, in any form or by any means, without permission.

First published 1979
by G. Solomons

Published 1980 by
Macmillan Education Ltd
London and Basingstoke
Associated companies and
representatives throughout
the world

Reprinted with corrections 1981

Typeset in 8/8 Univers by
STYLESET LIMITED
Salisbury · Wiltshire

Printed in Hong Kong

ABOUT SPELL IT

THE BOOK
This book contains 8000 words, which were carefully selected as those most frequently used by pupils of up to Secondary School age. Analysis has shown that it will contain most of the entire written vocabulary in normal use by these age groups. The book is intended to fit into pencil-case or pocket, and to be used wherever pupils do written work.

CONTENTS
Besides the word list, there is a place for personal details — timetable, peg or locker number, and so on — lists of names and places, and pages are provided for the recording of spellings of words not in 'SPELL IT'.

WORD ORDER
The words are arranged in alphabetical order, except where, in a few cases, it is more logical to arrange them differently. Words beginning with silent letters are also found in the place where they would appear if the silent letter were absent. Here, they are distinguished by brackets.

WORD ENDINGS
Regular past and continuous tenses (adding -ed and -ing to words such as walk, for example,) are not given, but all others are. Simple plurals, too, are not given except in cases where mistakes are commonly made. (monkey, monkeys is an example).

ALTERNATIVE SPELLINGS
Usually one spelling is given, that which is considered to be most frequently used in modern journalism and literature. Where alternative spellings are widely separated, (gipsy, gypsy), both appear.

MEANINGS OF WORDS
Very brief meanings are given where words sound alike (homophones) or are often confused (snack, snake).

FINALLY
SPELL IT used regularly, must help to improve spelling. Words *written* correctly first time are *learned* correctly. Practise this simple method of learning to spell.
1. Look at the word
2. Cover it up
3. Write the word
4. Check the spelling

ACKNOWLEDGEMENT

I should like to thank Mr. M. J. Hayhoe, MA, Senior Lecturer in English, Keswick Hall College of Education, Norwich, for his invaluable help and advice in the compiling of **Spell It**.

G. Solomons

NAME _____ **FORM** _____

SCHOOL _____

	1	2	3	4	5	6	7	8
M								
Tu								
W								
Th								
F								

_____
_____
_____
_____
_____
_____
_____
_____
_____

ABANDON

abandon
ability, abilities
able
aboard
abolish
about
above
abroad
abrupt
absence, absent
absolute
absurd
abuse, abusing, abusive
academic
accelerate, accelerating,
    acceleration, accelerator
accent
accept
access
accessory, accessories
accident, accidental,
    accidentally
accommodate, accommodating,
    accommodation
accompany, accompanied,
    accompanies, accompanying
accomplice
according
account
accumulate, accumulating,
    accumulation
accurate, accuracy
accuse, accusing, accusation
ace
ache, aching
achieve, achieving,
    achievement
acid
acknowledge, acknowledgement
acorn
acquaint, acquaintance
acquit, acquittal
acre
acrobat, acrobatic
across

AGENT

act, actor, actress
action
active
activity, activities
actual, actually
acute
adapt
add, addition
address
adequate
adhesive, adhesion
adjust, adjustable,
    adjustment
administer, administration
admire, admiring, admiration
admit, admission, admittance
adopt
adore, adoring, adorable
adrift
adult
advance, advancing
advantage
adventure, adventurous
advertise, advertisement,
    advertising
advice (my advice)
advise (I advise) advisable,
    advising
aerial
aeroplane, aerodrome
aerosol
affair
affect ('it will affect' — see also
    effect), affecting
affection, affectionate
afford
afloat
afraid
afresh
after, afterwards
afternoon
again, against
age, aged, aging
agency
agent

AGGRAVATE

aggravate, aggravating, aggravation
aggressive, aggressor
agile, agility
agitate, agitation, agitating, agitator
ago
agony
agree, agreement, agreeable
agriculture, agricultural
aground
ahead
aid
aim
air, airtight, airy
aircraft, airliner, airport, airship, airplane (see also words beginning aer-)
aisle
ajar
alarm, alarm-clock
album
alcohol, alcoholic
ale
algebra
alias
alibi
alight
alike
alive
all, all right
allergy, allergic
alley, alleyway
alligator
allot, allotment
allow, allowance
allowed (permitted — see also aloud)
almighty
almond
aloft
alone
along, alongside
aloud (with noise — see also allowed)

ANONYMOUS

alphabet, alphabetic, alphabetically
already
also
altar (in church)
alter (change)
alternate, alternately, alterna 
although
altogether
aluminium
always
amateur
amaze, amazing, amazement
ambassador
amber
ambition, ambitious
ambulance
ambush
ammunition
among, amongst
amount
ample, amply
amplify, amplified, amplifie 
amputate
amuse, amusement, amusing
anaesthetic
analyse, analysing, analysis
anatomy
ancestor, ancestral
anchor
ancient
angel, angelic (heavenly — s  also angle)
anger, angry
angle (an amount of turn, o  fish — see also angel), an 
animal
ankle
annihilate, annihilation
anniversary, anniversaries
announce, announcement, announcer
annoy, annoyance
annual
anonymous

ANORAK

anorak
another
answer
ant (insect — see also aunt)
antarctic
antenna, antennae
anthem
anticipate, anticipating, anticipation
antics
antidote
antique
antiseptic
anvil
anxious, anxiety
any, anybody, anyhow, anyone, anything, anywhere, anyway
apart, apartment
ape
apex
apology, apologise, apologising, apologetic
apparatus
apparent
appeal
appear, appearance
appendicitis
appendix
appetite, appetising
applaud, applause
apple
appliance
apply, application, applicant
appoint, appointment
appreciate, appreciation
apprentice, apprenticeship
approach
appropriate
approve, approval
approximate, approximately
apricot
apron
aqualung
aquarium

ASPHALT

arc (part of circle — see also ark)
arcade
arch, archbishop
architect, architecture
arctic
arduous
are, aren't
area
arena
argue, argument, argumentative
arise
aristocrat, aristocracy
arithmetic
ark (a vessel or chest — see also arc)
arm, armchair, armful
armour, armoury
arms, armament
army, armies
aroma, aromatic
around
arrange, arranging, arrangement
arrears
arrest
arrive, arrival, arriving
arrow
arsenal
arsenic
arson
art, artful
article
artificial
artillery
artist, artistic
asbestos
ascend, ascent
ash
ashamed
ashore
aside
ask
asleep
asphalt

ASPIRIN

aspirin
ass
assassin, assassinate
assault
assemble, assembly, assemblies
assess, assessment
assist, assistance, assistant
associate, association, associating
assortment
assure, assurance
asthma
astonish, astonishment
astray
astrologer (fortune teller — see also astronomer), astrology
astronaut
astronomer (scientist — see also astrologer), astronomy
asylum
athlete, athletic
atlas
atmosphere, atmospheric
atom, atomic
atrocious
attachment
attack
attain, attainment
attempt
attend, attendance, attendant
attention, attentive
attic
attitude
attract, attraction, attractive
auburn
auction, auctioneer
audible
audience
audition
aunt (parent's sister — see also ant)
authentic
author

BAGGAGE

authority, authorise
autobiography
autograph
automatic, automatically
automobile
autumn
auxiliary, auxiliaries
available
avalanche
avenge, avenging
avenue
average
aviation
avoid, avoidance
awake, awaken, awoke
award
aware
away
awful
awkward
axe
axis
axle

B

babble
baboon
baby, babies, babyish, babysitter
bachelor
bacillus, bacilli
back, backward, backwards
backbone
background
bacon
bacteria
bad
badge
badger
badminton
baffle, baffling
bag
baggage

BAGPIPE

bagpipes
bail (1. a bond 2. cricket — see also bale)
bait
bake, bakehouse, bakery
balance, balancing
balcony, balconies
bald
bale (1. bundle 2. ladle out water — see also bail)
ball, ball-bearing (see also bawl)
ballet
balloon
ballot
bamboo
ban
banana
band
bandage, bandaging
bandit
bang
bangle
banish, banishment
banisters
banjo, banjos
bank
bankrupt
banner
banquet
baptise, baptism
bar, barred
barb
barbecue
barber
bare (plain or naked — see also bear)
bargain
barge
bark
barley
barn
barnacle
barometer
baron, baroness, baronet

BEAUTY

barracks
barrage
barrel
barricade
barrier
barrow
barter
base, baseboard
baseball
basement
basic, basically
basin, basinful
basket
baste
bat, batting, batsman
batch
bath, bathing, bathroom (see also bathe)
bathe (to take a bath — see also bath)
batter
battery
battle, battling, battlefield, battleship, battlement
bawl (to shout — see also ball)
bay
bayonet
bazaar
beach (seashore — see also beech)
beacon
bead
beagle
beak
beaker
beam
bean, beanpole, beanstalk
bear (to carry, to suffer; animal — see also bare)
beard
bearing
beast
beat
beauty, beautiful, beautify, beautified

BECAME

became, become
because
bed
bee
beech (tree — see also beach)
beef, beefsteak
beer
beetroot
beetle
before, beforehand
beg, beggar, begged, begging
began, begin, beginner, begun
behave, behaviour, behaving
behead
behind
being
belfry, belfries
believe, belief, believing
bell
bellow (shout — see also below)
bellows
belong, belonging
below (underneath — see also bellow)
bench
bend
beneath
benefit, benefiting, benefited
benevolent
beret
berry, berries
berth (resting place — see also birth)
beside, besides
best
bet, betting
betray
better
bevel, bevelled
beware
bewildered
beyond
bible
bicycle
bid

BLISTER

big
bikini
bill
billiards
billion
bin
bind, binder, binding
binoculars
biography
biology
birch
bird
birth, birthday (see also berth)
biscuit
bisect
bishop
bit, bitten
bite
bitter
black
blackberry, blackberries
blackbird
blackboard
blackcurrant
blackleg
blackmail
blacksmith
bladder
blade
blame
blank
blanket, blanketed
blast
blaze
blazer
bleach
bleak
bleat
bleed, bled
blend
bless
blew (a blast — see also blue)
blind
blink
blister

BLIZZARD

blizzard
block
blockade
blockboard
blond (man) blonde (woman)
blood, bloodhound,
    bloodthirsty
bloom
blossom
blot, blotted, blotting,
    blotting-paper
blouse
blow, blown
blue (colour — see also blew)
bluebell, bluebottle
blunt
blur, blurred
blush
bluster
board, boarding-house,
    boarding-school
boast, boastful
boat
bob, bobbed, bobbing
bobbin
bobby
body, bodies, bodywork
bodyguard
bog, bogged, boggy
boil
boiler
bold, boldness
bolt
bomb, bomber
bombard, bombardment
bond
bone
bonfire
bonnet
bonus, bonuses
book, bookcase, bookmark
    bookshop
book-keeper, book-keeping
booklet
boom

BREATHE

boomerang
boot
border
bore, boring, boredom
born
borough
borrow
botany
both
bother
bottle
bottom
bough (of a tree — see also bow)
bought (past of buy)
boulder
bounce, bouncing
bound, boundary
bouquet (of flowers)
boutique (shop)
bow (curve, weapon, front of
    ship etc. — see also bough)
bowl, bowler
box
boy
brace
bracelet
braces
bracket
braid
brain, brainwave, brainwash
brake
branch
brand
brandy
brass
brave, bravery
braze, brazen, brazing
bread, breadboard, breadknife
breadth
break, breakable, breakage
breakdown
breakfast
breast
breath
breathe

BREECH

breech (of a gun)
breed, bred
breeze
brew, brewer, brewery
bribe, bribery
brick, bricklayer, brickwork
bride, bridal, bridesmaid
bridegroom
bridge
bridle (harness — see also bridal)
brief, briefly
brigade
bright
brilliant, brilliance
brim
bring, brought
brink
brisk
bristle
brittle
broad, broadcast, broadside
brocade
broke, broken
bronze
brooch
brood
brook
broom, broomstick
brother, brother-in-law
brought (past of bring)
brown
brownie
bruise
brunette
brunt
brush
brute, brutal, brutish
bubble, bubbling
buck
bucket, bucketful
buckle, buckling
bud, budded, budding
budge, budging

BUZZ

budgerigar
budget
buffer
buffet
bug
bugle
build, builder, building, built
bulb
bulge, bulging
bulk
bull, bulldog, bulldozer
bullet
bulletin
bullfinch
bullion
bullock
bull's-eye
bully, bullies, bullied
bump, bumper
bun
bunch
bundle, bundling
bungalow
bunk
bunker
buoy
burden
bureau, bureaux
burglar
burn, burned, burnt
burr
burrow
burst
bury, buried, burial
bus, buses
bush
business
busy
butcher
butler
butter, buttercup, butterfly
button
buy, bought
buzz

CAB

C

cab
cabbage
cabin
cabinet
cable
cackle
cactus, cacti
caddie (golf)
caddy (tea)
café
cafeteria
cage
cake
calculate, calculator
calendar
calf, calves
call, calling
calm
came
camel
camera, cameraman
camouflage
camp
campaign
can
canal
canary, canaries
cancel, cancelled, cancelling, cancellation
cancer
candidate
candle
candy, candied
cane
cannibal
cannon
cannot, can't
canoe
canopy
can't, cannot
canteen
canvas

CASUAL

cap
capable
capacity
cape
caper
capital
capsize
capsule
captain
captive
capture, capturing
car
caramel
caravan
carbon
carburettor
carcase or carcass
card, cardboard
cardigan
care, careful, carefree, careless
career, careers
caretaker
cargo, cargoes
carol, carolling
carp
carpenter, carpentry
carpet
carriage
carrier
carrot
carry, carried, carries, carrying
cart
carton
cartoon
cartridge
carve, carving
case
cash, cashier
cask
casserole
cassette
cast
castaway
castle
casual

CASUALTY

casualty
cat
catalogue
catapult
catarrh
catastrophe
catch, caught
caterpillar
cathedral
cattle
caught, catch
cauliflower
cause (make happen — see also course)
caution, cautious
cavalry
cave, cavern, caving
cavity, cavities
cease
ceiling
celebrate, celebration, celebrity
cell
cellar
cement
centenary
centigrade, centimetre, centipede
centre, central
century, centuries
cereal
ceremony
certain
certificate, certify, certified
chain
chair
chairman
chalet
chalk
challenge
champagne
champion, championship
chance
change, changing, changeable
channel

CHIP

chant
chaos, chaotic
chap, chapped
chapel
chapter
character
charcoal
charge, charging
charity, charities
charm, charming
chart
chase, chasing
chassis
chat, chatter
chauffeur
cheap
cheat
check, (examine closely — see also cheque)
check-out
check-point
cheek, cheeky, cheekily
cheer, cheerful, cheerfully
cheese
chef
chemical
chemist, chemistry
cheque (order for payment — see also check)
cherry, cherries
chess, chessboard, chessman
chest
chestnut
chew
chicken, chicken-pox
chief
chilblain
child, children, childish
chill, chilly
chime, chiming
chimney, chimneys
chimp, chimpanzee
chin
china
chip

CHISEL

chisel, chiselled, chiselling
chocolate
choice
choir, chorus, choral
choke
choose, choosing
chorus, choral
chose
christen, christening
Christian, Christianity
Christmas
chromium, chrome
chronic
chrysalis
chubby
chuckle, chuckling
chum
chunk
church, churchyard
cider
cigar, cigarette
cinder
cinema
circle, circular
circumference
circus
cistern
city, citizen, citizenship
civil, civility, civilised
civilian
claim
clamp
clang
clank
clap, clapped, clapping
clasp
class, classroom
classify, classification
clatter
claw
clay
clean, cleanliness
clear, clearway
clench
clergyman

COD

clerk
clever
click
client
cliff
climate
climb
cling
clinic
clip
cloak
clock, clockwork
clod
clog
close, closing, closure
clot
cloth (material — see also clothe, clothes)
clothe (to dress) clothes, clothing (garments)
cloud, cloudy, cloudless
clown
club
clue
clump
clumsy, clumsiness
cluster
clutch
clutter
coach
coal
coarse (rough — see also course, cause)
coast, coastal, coastguard
coaster
coax
cobbler
cobra
cobweb
cock, cockerel
cockpit
cocoa
coconut
cocoon
cod, codfish

CODE

code
coffee
coffin
cog
coil
coin, coinage, coiner
coincidence
coke
cold
collage (a decoration)
collapse, collapsible
collar
colleague
collect, collection, collector
college (a place of education)
collide, colliding, collision
collie
colony, colonial
colossal
colour, colourful, colourless
column
comb, combed, combing
combat
combine, combining, combination
come, coming
comedian
comedy, comedies
comet
comfort, comfortable
comic, comical
command, commander
commando, commandos
comment, commentator
commit
committee
common
commonwealth
commotion
communicate, communication
community, communities
compact
companion
company
compare, comparing

CONSIDER

compartment (a division — see also department)
compass (for directions)
compasses (for circles)
compel, compelled, compelling
compete, competition, competitor
complain, complaint
complete, completing, completion
complexion
complicate, complicated
compliment, complimentary
comprehend, comprehension
comprehensive
compress, compression, compressor
compulsory, compulsion
computer
conceal, concealment
concentrate, concentration
concern
concert
conclude, conclusion
concrete
concussion
condemn, condemnation
condense, condenser
condition
conduct, conductor
cone, conical
confectioner, confectionery
confess, confession
confetti
confidence, confidential
confiscate
confuse, confusing, confusion
congratulate, congratulating, congratulation
conjure, conjuror
conscience, conscientious
conscious, consciousness
consecutive
consequence
consider

CONSIDERABLE

considerable
consist
conspicuous
constable
constellation
construct, construction
consult, consultation
consume, consumption
contact, contact lenses
contain, container
contents
contest
continue, continuing
continual
continuous
contraband
contract
contractor
contrary
contrast
contribute, contribution
control, controlled, controlling
convenient, convenience
conversation
convex
convict, conviction
convince, convincing
convoy
cook, cookery
cool, coolly, coolness
co-operate, co-operating, co-operation
co-operative
copper
copy, copies
cord
cordon
core
cork, corkscrew
corn
corner
cornet
cornflakes, cornflour
coronation
correct, correction

CRASH

correspond, correspondence, correspondent
corridor
corrugated
cost
costume
cosy, cosier
cot
cottage
cotton
couch
cough, cough-medicine
could, couldn't
council, councillor
count, countless
counter
counterfeit
counterfoil
country, countries
county, counties
couple, coupling
coupon
courage
course (a series of lessons, a track or a movement. See also coarse, cause)
court, courtyard
courtesy, courteous
cousin
cover
cow
coward, cowardice
cowboy
crab
crack
cracker
crackle, crackling
cradle
craft, craftsman, craftsmanship
crafty, craftily
cram, cramming
cramp
crane
crank
crash

CRATE

crate
crater
crawl
crayon
craze, crazy, crazily
creak
cream
crease, creasing
create, creating, creator, creation, creative
creature
credit, creditor
creep, crept
crest
crew
crib, cribbed
cricket
cried
crime, criminal
crimson
cripple
crisis
crisp
critic, criticise, criticism
critical
croak
crockery
crocodile
crook, crooked
crop, cropping, cropped
cross, crossbow, crossroads
crow, crowed
crowbar
crowd
crown
crude
cruel, cruelty
cruise, cruising
crumb
crumble, crumbling
crumple, crumpling
crunch
crush
crust
crutches

DAGGER

cry, cried, cries
crystal
cub
cube, cubic
cubicle
cuckoo
cucumber
cuddle, cuddling
cue
cuff
culprit
cultivate, cultivation
culture
cunning
cup, cupful
cupboard
curdle
cure, curing
curious, curiosity
curl
currant (fruit — see also current)
currency
current (flow — see also currant)
curse, cursing
curtain
curve, curving
cushion
custard
custody
custom, customer
cut
cutler
cycle, cycling
cylinder, cylindrical

D

dab
dabble
dad, daddy
daffodil
dagger

DAILY

daily
dainty
dairy (milk shop — see also diary)
daisy
dam
damage, damaging
damp
dance, dancing
dandelion
danger, dangerous
dangle
dare, daring, daredevil
dark, darkness
darling
darn
dart
dash
dashboard
data
date
daub
daughter
dawdle
dawn
day, daylight, daytime
daze
dazzle
dead, deaden, deadly
deaf, deafness, deafening
deal, dealer
dear
death
debt
decay
deceit, deceitful, deceive
decent
deceptive
decide, decision
decimal
deck
declare, declaration
decorate, decoration, decorator
decoy
deduce, deduction

DERELICT

deduct
deed
deep
deer
deface
defeat
defect, defective
defence, defenceless, defensive
defend
definite, definitely
defy, defiance
degree
dejected, dejection
delay
deliberate, deliberately
delicate, delicacy
delicious
delight, delightful
delinquent, delinquency
delirious
delivery
demand
democracy, democrat
demolish, demolition
demon
demonstrable
demonstrate, demonstrator, demonstration
den
denim
dense
dent
dental
dentist
deny, denial
depart, departure
department (part of a store etc. — see also compartment)
depend
deposit
depot
depth
deputy, deputies
derelict

DESCEND

descend, descent, descendant
describe, describing, description
    descriptive
desert (run away, or waste-land.
    See also dessert)
deserve
design, designer
desire, desirable, desiring
desk
despair, desperate
despatch
desperate
despise, despising, despicable
dessert (food after main course
    — see also desert)
destination
destroy, destroyer
destruction, destructive
detail
detain
detect, detective, detector
detention
detergent
determine
detest
detonate, detonator
devastate, devastation
develop, development
device
devil
devoted
dew
diagnose, diagnosis
diagonal
diagram
dial, dialled, dialling
dialect
diameter
diamond
diarrhoea
diary (a daily record — see
    also dairy)
dice
dictate, dictation, dictator
dictionary, dictionaries

DISLIKE

did, didn't
die, dying (of death — see
    also dye)
diesel
diet
differ, different, difference
difficult, difficulty
dig, digging, dug
digest, digestion, digestive
dignified
dignity
dilapidated
dilute
dim
din
dine, dining
dinner
dinosaur
dip
direct, direction
director
directory
dirt, dirty, dirtier
disagree, disagreement
disappear, disappearance
disappoint, disappointment
disaster
disbelieve
disc, disco, discotheque
discipline
disconnect
discount
discover, discovery
discus (a disc)
discuss (talk)
disease
disgrace, disgraceful
disguise
disgust
dish
dishonest
disinfect, disinfectant
disintegrate
disk
dislike

DISMAL

dismal
dismay
disobedience, disobedient
dispatch
disperse
dispose, disposal
disqualify, disqualified, disqualification
dissolve, dissolving
distance, distant
distinct, distinction
distinguish
distract
distress
distribute, distribution
district
disturb, disturbance
ditch
divan
dive, diving
diversion, divert
divide, dividing, division
divorce
dizzy
do, don't, done
    does, doesn't
dock
doctor
document, documentary
dodge, dodging
dog
dole
doll, dolly, dollies
dollar
dome
domestic, domesticate
donate, donation
donkey, donkeys
door, doorway
dormitory
dose
dot, dotted
double
doubt, doubtful
dough, doughnut

DULL

down, downstairs
doze
dozen
drag, dragged, dragging
dragon, dragonfly
drain
drama, dramatic
drank (see also drink)
drape
draught, draughts, draughty
draw (to pull, or picture — see also drawer and drawers)
    drawing, drawn
drawer (sliding container)
drawers (underclothes)
dread, dreadful
dream
dreary
dress, dressing-gown
dresser
drew
dried
drift
drill
drink, drank, drunk
drip, dripped, dripping
drive, driver, driven, driving
drizzle
drop, dropped, dropping
drought
drove
drown
drowsy
drug, drugged
drum, drummer
drunk (see also drink)
drunkard, drunken
dry, dried, drier
duck
due
duel, duelling
duet
duffel coat
dug
dull

DUMB

dumb, dumbfounded
dummy, dummies
dump, dumper
dune
dungarees
dungeon
duplicate, duplicating, duplicator
during
dust
duty, duties
dwarf
dwelling
dye (colour) dyeing, dyed
dying (death)
dynamite
dynamo, dynamos

E

each
eager
eagle
ear
early, earlier
earn, earning
earth, earthquake
ease, easy, easily, easier
east, eastern
easy
eat, eaten, eatable
eccentric
echo, echoes
economy, economise
edge
edible
edit, editor
educate, education, educating
eel
effect ('the effect was — see also affect) effective
efficient, efficiency
effort
egg, eggshell

ENTITLE

eight, eighteen, eighth, eighty
either
eject, ejection
elastic
elbow
elder, elderly
elect, election, elector
electric, electrical, electricity, electrician
elegant, elegance
elephant
elevator
eleven, eleventh
eliminate, elimination
elm
else, elsewhere
embarrass, embarrassment
embassy
embroider, embroidery
emerald
emerge, emerging
emergency, emergencies
emigrate, emigrant
emotion, emotional
emphasis, emphasize
employ, employment, employee, employer
empty, empties
endanger
endure, endurance
enemy, enemies
energy, energies, energetic, energetically
engage, engagement
engine, engineer
enjoy, enjoyment
enormous
enough
enquire, enquiry
enter, entry
entertain, entertainment
enthusiasm, enthusiast, enthusiastically
entire, entirely
entitle, entitlement

ENTRANCE

entrance, entrant
entry, entries
envelope
envy, envies, envious
epidemic
episode
equal, equalled, equality
equator
equilateral
equip, equipment
equivalent, equivalence
erase, erasing, eraser
errand
erratic, erratically
error
erupt, eruption
escalator
escape, escaping
escort
essay
essential, essentially
establishment
estate
estimate, estimating
evacuate, evacuating,
    evacuation, evacuee
evaporate, evaporating,
    evaporation
eve, evening
even
event, eventful
eventual, eventually
ever
every, everybody, everyone,
    everything, everywhere
evidence
evident, evidently
evil
exact
exaggerate, exaggerating,
    exaggeration
examine, examining,
    examination
example
excavate, excavation

EXTRA

excellent
except, exception
exchange, exchanging
excite, exciting, excitement
exclaim, exclamation
exclude, exclusion
exclusive
excursion
excuse, excusing
execute, executing, execution
executive
exempt, exemption
exercise
exhaust
exhibit, exhibition
exile
exist, existence
exit
exotic
expand, expansion
expect, expectant
expedition
expel, expelled, expelling,
    expulsion
expenditure
expense, expensive
experience
experiment
expert
expire, expiry
explain, explanation
explode, exploding,
    explosion, explosive
explore, exploration, explorer
export
expose, exposing
express, expression,
    expressive
expulsion
extend, extension, extent
exterior
exterminate, extermination
extinct
extinguish, extinguisher
extra

EXTRACT

extract, extraction
extraordinary
extravagant, extravagance
extreme
eye, eyebrow, eyelash, eyesight

F

(See also words beginning
    with ph—)
fable
fabric
fabulous
face, facing
fact
factory, factories
fad
fade, fading
fail, failure
faint
fair (not dark, pleasure ground,
    just — see also fare)
fairground
faith, faithful
fake
fall, fallen, fall-out
false
fame, famous
familiar
family, families
famine
famous
fan, fanned, fanning
fanatic, fanatical
fancy, fancies
fang
fantastic
far, farfetched
fare (cost of travel — see also
    fair)
farewell
farm, farmer
farther (more distant — see
    also father)

FIERCE

fascinate, fascinating,
    fascination
fashion, fashionable
fast, fasten
fat, fatter, fatten
fatal, fatality
fate, fateful
father (male parent — see also
    farther) father-in-law
fatigue, fatiguing
fault, faulty
favour, favourite, favouritism
fear, fearful, fearless
feast
feat
feather
feature
fee
feeble
feed, fed
feel, feeler, feeling
feet
fell
fellow
felt
female, feminine
fence, fencing
fend, fender
fern
ferocious, ferocity
ferry, ferried, ferries
fertile, fertility
festival
fetch
fête
feud
fever
few
fib
fibre
fiction, fictitious
fiddle
fidget
field
fierce

FIERY

fiery
fifteen, fifteenth, fifth, fifty
fig
fight, fighter
figure, figuring
file, filed, filing
fill, full
fillet, filleted
filling
film
filter
filth, filthy, filthier
fin
final, finally
finance, financial
find
fine
finger, finger-print
finish
fir (tree — see also fur)
fire, fiery
fire-arms
fireproof, fireworks
firm
first, first-class
fish, fisherman
fist
fit, fitted, fitting
five
fix
fixture
fizz
flag, flagging
flagrant
flake, flaking
flame, flaming
flank
flannel
flap, flapped, flapping
flare, flaring
flash, flashback
flask
flat
flatter, flattery
flavour, flavouring

FOLD

flea (insect — see also flee)
fleck
flee (run away — see also flea)
    fled
fleece, fleecy, fleecing
fleet
flesh
flew (past of fly — see also
    'flu, flue)
flexible, flexibility
flick, flicker
flight
flimsy
fling, flung
flint
flip, flipped, flipping
flirt
float
flock
flog, flogged, flogging
flood
floor
flop, flopped, flopping
florist
flour (meal — see also flower)
flow
flower (blossom — see also
    flour)
flown
'flu (illness — see also flue,
    flew)
flue (smoke stack — see also
    'flu, flew)
fluent, fluently
fluff
fluid
fluorescence, fluorescent
flush
flutter
fly, flew, flown, flies, flyover
foam
focus, focuses, focusing
fog, foggy, foggier
foil
fold

FOLDER

folder
folk
follow
fond
food
fool, foolish, foolishness
foot, feet
football
footpath
footprint
footstep
for
forbid, forbidden
force
ford
forearm
forecast
forehead
foreign, foreigner
foreman
forest
forever
forfeit
forge, forging
forgery
forget, forgetting, forgot, forgotten
forgive, forgiving, forgiveness
forgot, forgotten
fork
form
formal
former, formerly
formula, formulae
fort
fortnight
fortune, fortunate, fortunately
forty
forward
fossil
foster
fought
foul (dirty — see also fowl)
found
foundation

FROTH

foundry
fountain
four, fourth
fourteen, fourteenth
fowl (bird — see also foul)
fox
fraction
fracture, fracturing
fragile, fragility
fragment
frail
frame, framing
franc (French coin — see also frank)
frank (to stamp, or outspoken — see also franc)
frantic, frantically
fraud, fraudulent
fray
freak
freckles
free, freedom, freely
freeze
freight
frenzy, frenzied
frequent, frequently
fresh
fret, fretted, fretting
fretwork, fretsaw
friction
fridge
fried
friend, friendly, friendliness, friendship
fright
frighten, frightened
frill
fringe
frock
frog, frogman
from
front
frontier
frost
froth

FROWN

frown
froze, frozen
fruit, fruitful
frustrate, frustrated, frustration
fry, fried
fuel, fuelled, fuelling
fugitive
full
fumble, fumbling
fume, fuming
fun, funfair
function
fund
funeral
fungus, fungi
funnel
funny, funnier, funniest
fur (animals' coats — see also fir)
furious
furnace
furnish
furniture
further
fury, furious
fuse, fusing
fuselage
fuss
future, futuristic

G

(See also words beginning with j-)
gabble, gabbling
gadget
gag, gagged, gagging
gain
gala
galaxy
gale
gallant
gallon
gallows

GIFT

galvanise
gamble, gambling
game
gang, gangster
gangway
gaol
gap
gape, gaping
garage
garbage
garden, gardener
gargle, gargling
garlic
garment
gas, gases, gassed, gassing
gash
gasp
gate
gather
gauge, gauging
gauze
gave
gay, gaily
gaze, gazing
gear, gearbox, gearlever
geese
gelatine
gem
general, generally
generate, generator, generation
generous, generosity
genius, geniuses
gentle, gentleman
genuine
geography
geology
geometry
germ, germinate
gesture
get, got, getting
ghastly
ghost, ghostly
giant, gigantic
giddy, giddily, giddier
gift, gifted

GIGANTIC

gigantic
giggle, giggling
gill
gilt
gimmick
gin
ginger, gingerbread,
  gingersnap
gipsy, gipsies
girder
girl
give, giving, given, gave
glad
glamour, glamorous
glance, glancing
gland, glandular
glare, glaring
glass, glassful
glaze, glazing
gleam
glide, glider, gliding
glimpse, glimpsing
glint
glitter
gloat
globe
gloom, gloomier
glory, glorious
gloss, glossy, glossiness
glove
glow
glue, gluing
glutton, gluttony
gnaw
go, goes, gone, going
goal, goalie, goalkeeper
goat
gobble, gobbling
God
god, gods, goddess
gold, golden
golf, golfball
gone
gong
good, good-bye, good-hearted

GREENGROCER

good-looking, good-natured
goose, geese
gooseberry, gooseberries
gorgeous
gorilla (ape — see also guerilla)
gossip
got
govern, government
governor
gown
grab, grabbed, grabbing
grace, graceful, gracious
grade, grading
gradual, gradually
graft
grain
gram, gramme
grammar
grand
grandchild, grandchildren
grand-daughter, grandson
grandfather, grandpa
grandmother, grandma,
  granny, grannies
granite
grant
grape, grapefruit
graph
grasp
grasshopper
grate (fireplace, or to scrape —
  see also great)
grateful, gratefully
grating
gratitude
grave, graveyard
gravel
gravity
gravy
graze, grazing
grease, greasy
great (very big — see also grate)
greedy
green
greengrocer, greengrocery

GREENHOUSE

greenhouse
greet
grenade
grew
grey
grid
grief
grieve, grievous, grievance
grill
grim
grin, grinned, grinning
grind
grip, gripped, gripping
gristle, gristly
grit
groan (a noise — see also grown)
grocer, grocery, groceries
groove
grotesque
ground
group
grouse
grow, grown, growth
growl
grown (become older,
  taller etc.) growth
grub
grubby
grudge, grudging
gruesome
gruff
grumble, grumbling
guarantee
guard, guardian
guerilla (fighter — see
  also gorilla)
guess, guesswork
guest
guide, guiding, guidance
guilt, guilty
guitar
gulp
gum, gummed
gun, gunboat, gunpowder, gunship
gurgle, gurgling

HAPPY

gust
gut, guts
gutter
guy
gym, gymnasium
gypsy

H

habit, habitual
hack, hacksaw
had, hadn't
haddock
hag
hail, hailstones
hair, hairy, hairier, hairdryer
half, halve, halves, halfpenny
hall (a large room or corridor
  — see also haul)
hallo or hello
halo
halt
halve, halves
ham, hamburger
hammer
hammock
hand, handful
handcuff
handicap, handicapped
handicraft
handkerchief, handkerchieves,
  hankie
handle, handle-bars
handsome
handwriting
handy, handier
hang, hanger (to hang with —
  see also hangar)
hangar (for aircraft — see also
  hanger)
haphazard
happen
happy, happily, happier,
  happiest, happiness

HARBOUR

harbour
hard, hardy
hardship
hardware
hardwood
hare (animal — see also hair)
harm, harmful, harmless
harmony, harmonise
harness
harp
harsh
harvest
has, hasn't
haste, hasty, hastily
hat
hatch
hatchet
hate, hateful, hating, hatred
haughty
haul (to drag — see also hall)
haunt, haunted
have, haven't, having
haversack
hawk
hay, haystack
hazard, hazardous
haze, hazy
hazel
head
headache
headlights
headline
headmaster, headmistress,
    head-teacher
headquarters
heal (to make better — see
    also heel)
health, healthy, healthier
heap
hear, heard
hearse
heart
heartbreak, heartbroken
heartless
heat

HIP

heave
heaven
heavy, heavier
hectare
hectic
hedge, hedgehog, hedging
heed
heel (of a shoe — see also heal)
height
heir, heiress, heirloom
held
helicopter
hell
hello or hallo
helmet
help, helpful, helpless
hem
hen
herb
herd
here
heritage
hermit, hermitage
hero, heroine, heroic, heroism
herring
hers
herself
hesitate
hibernate
hid, hidden
hide, hiding
hideous
high
highway, highwayman
hijack, hijacker
hike
hilarious
hill
hilt
himself
hind
hinder, hindrance
hinge, hinging
hint
hip

HIRE

hire, hiring
his
hiss
history, historic
hit
hitch
hive
hoard (of treasure — see also horde)
hoarse
hoax
hobble, hobbling
hobby, hobbies
hockey
hoe
hog
hoist
hold, held
(whole, wholly)
hole
holiday
hollow
holly
holster
holy, holier
home
homesick, homewards
homicide
honest, honesty
honey
honour, honourable
(who, who's = who is)
(whom, whose)
hood
hoof, hooves
hook
hooligan
hoop
(whooping cough)
hoot
hop, hopped, hopping
hope, hoping, hopeful, hopeless
horde (a mob — see also hoard)
horizon, horizontal
horn

HURRICANE

horrible
horrify, horrified
horror
horse, horse riding, horse-power
hose, hosing
hospitable, hospitality
hospital
host, hostess
hostage
hostel
hostile, hostility
hot
hotel
hound
hour, hourly
house, household, housing
housekeeper
housewife
hovel
hover, hovercraft
how, however
howl
hub
hubbub
huddle, huddling
hue
hug, hugged
huge
hull
hum, hummed
human
humble
humid
humour, humorous
hump
hunch, hunchback
hundred, hundredweight
hung
hunger, hungry
hunt, hunter
hurdle, hurdling
hurl
hurray
hurricane

HURRY

hurry, hurries, hurrying
hurt
husband
hush
husky
hut
hutch
hydraulic, hydro-electric
hydrogen
hygiene
hymn
hypnotise
hypocrite, hypocrisy
hysteria, hysterics

I

ice, icy, icily, icicle
iceberg
ice-cream
icicle
idea
ideal, ideally
identical, identically
identify, identifies, identified
identity, identities
idiot, idiotic
idle, idling, idly
idol
igloo
ignite, ignition
ignorant, ignorance
ignore
ill, illness
illegal
illegible
illiterate
illuminate, illumination
illustrate, illustration
image
imagine, imaginative, imaginary, imagination
imitate, imitation
immediate, immediately

INDOORS

immense
immigrant
immigrate, immigration
immune, immunise, immunity
impact
impatient, impatience
imperfect
impertinent
imply, implied
import
important
impress, impressive
improve, improvement, improving
impudent, impudence
impulse, impulsive
inaccurate, inaccuracy
inaudible
incapable
incense
incentive
inch
incident
incidental, incidentally
inclined
include, including
inclusive
income
incompetent, incompetence
incomplete
inconvenient, inconvenience
incorrect
increase
incredible, incredibly
incurable
indeed
independent, independence
index
indicate, indication, indicating
indigestion, indigestible
indignant, indignation
indirect
indistinct
individual
indoors

INDUSTRY

industry
inefficient
inertia
inevitable, inevitably
inexpensive
inexperienced
infamous
infant, infancy
infantry
infect, infection
inferior
infest
inflame, inflaming, inflammation
inflammable
inflate, inflating, inflatable
inflict
influence
influenza
inform, information
informal
infuriate, infuriating
ingenious, ingenuity
ingredient
inhabit, inhabitant
inhale, inhaling
inherit, inheritance
inhuman
initial
initiative
inject, injection
injure, injury
ink
inland
inn, inn-keeper
inner
innocent, innocence
inoculate, inoculation
inquest
inquire, inquiry, inquiring
inquisitive
insane, insanity
insect
insert
inside
insist

INVITE

insolent, insolence
inspect, inspector, inspection
    inspecting
install
instalment
instance
instant, instantly
instead
instinct, instinctive
instruct, instructor, instruction
instrument
insufficient
insulate, insulator, insulation
insult
insure, insuring, insurance
intelligent, intelligence
intend
intense, intensity
intensive
interest, interesting
interfere, interference
interior
intermediate
internal
international
interpret, interpreter,
    interpretation
interrupt, interruption
interval
interview
intimate
into
intoxicate, intoxicating,
    intoxication
introduce, introduction
intrude, intruder, intrusion
invade, invader, invasion
invalid
invaluable
invent, inventor, invention
investor
investigate, investigator,
    investigation
invisible, invisibility
invite, invitation, inviting

INVOLVE

involve, involving
inward
iron, ironmonger
irregular
irresponsible, irresponsibility
irrigate, irrigating, irrigation
irritate, irritating, irritation
is, isn't
island
isolate, isolation, isolating
issue
itch
item
its (belong to it) it's (it is)
ivory
ivy

J

(See also words beginning with g-)
jab, jabbed, jabbing
jabber
jack, jack-knife, jackpot
jacket
jagged
jail, jailer
jam, jammed, jamming
jar, jarred, jarring
jargon
javelin
jaw
jazz
jealous, jealousy
jeans
jeep
jeer
jelly, jellies
jerk
jersey, jerseys
jet, jet-propelled
jewel, jeweller, jewellery
jig-saw
job

KETCHUP

jockey
jog, jogged, jogging
join
joint
joke, joking
jolly
jolt
jostle
jot
journal, journalist
journey, journeys
joy, joyful
judge, judging
judo
jug
juggle, juggler
juice, juicy
juke-box
jumble
jump
junction
jungle
junior
junk
jury
just
justice
justify
jut, jutted, jutting
juvenile

K

(See also words beginning with with c- or q-)
karate
keel
keen
keep, keeper
keg
kennel
kept
kerb
ketchup

KETTLE

kettle
key, keyhole
khaki
kick
kid
kidnap, kidnapper, kidnapped
kidney
kill
kiln
kilogram
kilometre
kilt
kind, kindness, kindly
kindle
king
kiosk
kipper
kiss
kit
kitchen, kitchenette
kite
kitten
kitty
knack
knead (dough — see also need)
knee, kneel, knelt
knew
knickers
knife, knives
knight (man of rank, chessman — see also night)
knit, knitted, knitting
knob
knock
knocker
knot
know, knowledge, known
knuckle

L

label, labelling, labelled
laboratory, laboratories

LAWN

labour
labourer
lace
lack
lad
ladder
ladle
lady, ladies
lag
laid
lake
lamb
lame
lamp, lamp-post
land
landing
landlord
landowner
landslide
lane
language
lantern
lap
lapel
lard
larder
large
larva, larvae
laser
lash
lasso
last
latch
late
lathe
lather
latter
laugh, laughter
launch
laundry, laundrette
lava
lavatory
lavender
law, lawful, lawless
lawn

LAWYER

lawyer
lay
layer
lazy, lazier
lead, led
leader
leaf
leaflet
league
leak (drain away — see also leek)
lean
leap, leap-year
learn, learned
learning
lease, leasing
leash
least
leather
leave, leaving
lecture, lecturing
led
ledge
leek (vegetable — see also leak)
leer
left
leg
legacy
legal
legend, legendary
legible, legibility
legion
leisure, leisurely
lemon, lemonade
lend
length, lengthen
lenient
lens
lent
leopard
leper, leprosy
less, lessen
lesson
let
letter

LISP

lettuce
level, levelled, levelling
lever
liable, liability
liar
libel
liberate, liberating, liberation
liberty
library, librarian
licence (document giving permission — see also license)
license (to allow officially)
lick
licorice
lid
lie, liar, lying
lieutenant
life, lives, lifeless
lift
light
lighten
lighthouse
lightning
like, likeness
likely
limb
lime
limerick
limit, limited
limp
line, lining
linen
liner
linger
lingerie
lining
link
lino, linoleum, lino-tiles
lion
lip, lipstick
liquid
liquidate, liquidation
liquor, liquorice
lisp

LIST

list
listen, listener
lit
literature
litre
litter
little
live, living
liver
lives
livid
living
lizard
load
loaf, loaves
loan
loathe, loathsome
loaves
lobby, lobbies
lobster
local, locality
locate, locating, location
lock
locker
lodge, lodger
loft
lofty
log
logic, logical
loiter
lollipop, lolly
lone, lonely, lonelier
long, longing
longitude
look
loop
loose (not caught, or free —
  see also lose)
loot
lop
lord
lorry, lorries
lose, (to be beaten, or opposite
  of find — see also loose),
  loser, losing

MADE

loss
lost
lot
lottery
loud
lounge
love, loving, lovely
low
loyal
lubricate, lubrication
luck, lucky, luckily
ludicrous
luggage
lukewarm
lull
lullaby
lumbago
lumber
lumberjack
luminous
lump
lunar
lunatic
lunch
lung
lunge
lurch
lurid
lurk
luscious
luxurious, luxury
lying
lynch

M

macaroni
macaroon
machine, machinery
mackintosh, mac
mad, madness, madman
madam (English), madame
  (French)
made

MADEMOISELLE

mademoiselle
magazine
maggot
magic, magician
magistrate
magnet, magnetic, magnetise
magnificent, magnificence
mahogany
maid, maiden
mail, mail-order
maim
main (chief one — see also mane)
maintain, maintenance
majestic, majesty
major, majority
make, making
male
malice
mallet
malt
mammal
mammoth
man, men
manage, manager, manageress
mane (horse's hair — see also main)
mania, maniac
manicure
manipulate, manipulating, manipulation
mannequin
manner, manners
manoeuvre
manor
mansion
manslaughter
mantelpiece
manual
manufacture, manufacturing
manure
manuscript
many
map
marathon

MAYBE

marble
march
mare (female horse — see also mayor)
margarine
margin, marginal
marine
mark
market
marmalade
maroon
marriage
marrow
marry, married
marsh
marshal
martyr, martyrdom
marvel, marvellous
mascara
mascot
masculine
mash
mask
mass
massacre
massage
massive
mast
master
masterpiece
mat, matted, matting
match
mate
material
maternal, maternity
mathematics, mathematician, maths
matrimony, matrimonial
matter
mattress
mature
maul
maximum
may
maybe

MAYOR

mayor (chief citizen — see also mare) mayoress
maze
meadow
meal
mean, meanness, meant
meanwhile
measles
measure, measuring
meat
mechanical, mechanic, mechanism
medal (decoration — see also meddle)
meddle (interfere — see also medal)
medieval
medicine, medical
medium
medley
meek
meet, meeting, met
melody, melodies, melodious
melt
member, membership
memento
memory, memories, memorial, memorise
menace
menagerie
mend
mental, mentally, mentality
mention
menu
merchant, merchandise
mercury
mercy, mercies
mere
merge, merging, merger
merit
merry, merrily
mesh
mess
message
messenger

MISBEHAVE

met
metal, metallic
meteor, meteorite, meteorology
meter (gas-meter, etc. — see also metre)
method
metre (about 39 inches — see also meter) metric
mice
microbe
microfiche, microfilm
microphone, mike
microscope, microscopic
midday
middle, middle-aged
midge
midget
midnight
midst
might
migrate, migration
mild
mildew
mile, mileage
military
milk, milkman
mill
millimetre
million
millionaire
mince, mincing
mincemeat
mind
mine, mining
mineral
miniature
minibus
minimum
minister, ministry
mint
minus
minute
miracle, miraculous
mirror
misbehave, misbehaviour

35

MISCHIEF

mischief, mischievous
miser
miserable, misery
misfortune
miss, missed
missile
mission
mist
mistake, mistaken, mistook
mistletoe
mistook
mistress
mistrust
misunderstand, misunderstood
mitre
mix
mixture
moan
moat
mob
mobile, mobility
mock
model
moderate
modern, modernise
modest, modesty
module, modular
moist, moisture
mole
molecule, molecular
molten
moment, momentary
monastery
money
mongrel
monitor
monk
monkey, monkeys
monocle
monopoly
monotonous, monotony
monster, monstrous
month
monument
mood, moody

MUG

moon, moonlight
moor, moorland
mop, mopped, mopping
moped
moral, morals
morale
more
morning
morphia
morsel
mortar
mortgage
mosaic
mosque
mosquito
moss
most, mostly
motel
moth
mother, mother-in-law
motion, motionless
motive
motor, motor-boat,
    motor-cycle
motor-cycling
motorist
motorway
motto
mould, mouldy
moult
mound
mount, mountain
mountaineer, mountainous
mourn, mourning, mournful
mouse
moustache
mouth, mouthful
move, moveable, moving,
    movement
mow, mower, mown
much
mud, muddy
muddle
muffle
mug

MULE

mule
multiply, multiplied
mumble, mumbling
mummy, mummies
mumps
munch
mural
murder, murderous, murderer
murmur
muscle, muscular
museum
mushroom
music, musical, musician
must, mustn't
mustard
mutilate, mutilation
mutiny, mutineer, mutinied
mutter
mutton
mutual
muzzle
my
myself
mystery, mysteries, mysterious
myth
myxomatosis

N

Words in brackets sound as
though they begin with n-)
(knack)
nag, nagged, nagging
nail
naked
name
nap
napkin
narcotic
narrate, narration, narrator
narrow
nasty
nation, national

NICKEL

native
natural
nature, naturalist
naughty
navy, naval
(gnaw)
(knead) (dough — see also need)
near, nearly
neat
necessary
necessity, necessities
neck, necklace
(knee, kneel, knelt)
need (want — see also knead)
needle, needlework
negative
neglect, neglectful
negro, negroes, negress
neigh
neighbour, neighbourhood
neither
neon
nephew
nerve, nervous, nervousness
nest
net
network
nettle
neutral, neutrality
never, nevertheless
(knew) (past of know — see
  also new)
new (not old — see also knew)
(pneumatic)
(pneumonia)
news, newspaper, newsreader,
  newsflash
next
(knickers)
nib
nibble, nibbling
nice
nick
nickel

NICKNAME

nickname
niece
(knife, knives)
night, nightdress, nightmare, night-time (see also — knight)
nil
nine, nineteen, ninety, ninth
nip, nipped, nipping
(knit, knitted, knitting)
nitrogen
no
(knob)
noble, nobly
nobody
(knock, knocker)
nod, nodded, nodding
noise, noisy, noisily
none
nonsense
noon
noose
normal, normally
north, north-east, north-west
nose
nostril
(knot)
notable
notch
note, noting
nothing
notice, noticing, noticeable, noticeably
notify, notified, notifying, notification
notorious
nought
nourishment
novel, novelist
novelty, novelties
(know, knowledge, known)
now, nowadays
nowhere
nozzle
(knuckle)

OBVIOUS

nuclear, nucleus
nudge, nudging
nuisance
numb
number
numeral
numerous
nun, nunnery
nurse, nursing
nursery, nurseries
nut, nutty
nutrition, nutritious
nylon

O

(Words in brackets sound as though they begin with o-)

oak
oar
oasis
oath
oats
obedient, obedience
obey
object, objection, objectionable
objective
obligation, obligatory
oblige, obliging
oblique
obliterate
oboe
obscene, obscenity, obscenities
obscure, obscuring
observant
observation
observe
obsess, obsessed, obsession
obsolete
obstacle
obstinate, obstinacy
obstruct
obtain
obvious

OCCASION

occasion, occasional
occupation
occupy, occupied
occur, occurred, occurrence
ocean
o'clock
octopus
odd, oddity
odds
odious
odour
of
off
offence, offensive
offend
offer
offhand
office
officer
official
often
oil, oily
ointment
old, old-fashioned
olive
omelette
ominous
omission
omit, omitted, omitting
once
one
(honest, honesty)
onion
only
(honour, honourable)
onslaught
opaque
open
opening
openly
opera
operate, operating, operation, operator
opinion
opium

OUTLOOK

opponent
opportunity, opportunities
oppose, opposer, opposition
opposite
optician
optimist, optimistic, optimistically
option, optional
oral
orange
orang-utan
orbit, orbital, orbiting
orchard
orchestra
ordeal
order
ordinary
organ
organisation, organise
orgy
origin
original, originality
originate
ornament, ornamental
orphan, orphanage
(see also words beginning au-)
other, otherwise
ought
ounce
(hour, hourly)
our, ours, ourselves
out
outbreak
outcome
outcry
out-dated
outdoors
outer
outfit
outing
outlast
outlaw
outlay
outline
outlook

OUTNUMBER

outnumber, outnumbered
outpost
output
outrage, outrageous
outright
outside
outskirts
outspoken
outstanding
outward
outwit
oval
ovation
oven
over
overalls
overboard
overcast
overcharge, overcharging
overcome, overcoming, overcame
overcrowd
overdue
overflow
overgrown
overhaul
overhead
overhear, overheard
overjoyed
overlap, overlapped, overlapping
overload
overlook
overnight
overrule
overseas
overtake, overtook
overtime
overturn
overweight
overwhelm
overwork
owe
owl
own, owner, ownership
oxygen
oyster

PARASITE

P

pace
pack, package, packet, packaging
pact
pad, padded, padding
paddle
paddock
padlock
page
paid
pail, pailful
pain, painful, painless (see also pane)
paint
pair (two of a kind — see also pear)
palace
pale
palm
pamper
pamphlet
pan, pancake
panda
pandemonium
pane (of glass — see also pain)
panel, panelled, panelling, panellist
pang
panic
panorama, panoramic
pant
panther
pantomime
pantry
pants
paper, paperback
parachute, parachuting
parade, parading
paradise
paraffin
paragraph
parallel
paralyse, paralysis
parapet
parasite, parasitic

PARATROOPS

paratroops, paratrooper
parcel, parcelled, parcelling
parchment
pardon
parent, parental
parish
park
parliament
parole
parrot
parson
part, partial, partly
participate
particular
partition
partner, partnership
party, parties
pass
passage
passed ('I passed him' — see also past)
passenger
passion, passionate
passport
past ('walked past', 'half past one', 'in the past' — see also passed)
paste, pasting
pastel
pastry, pastries
pasture
pat
patch, patchwork
patent
path
pathetic
patience, patient
patrol
pattern
pause
pave, pavement
pavilion
paw
pay, payment, pay-packet, payroll
pea

PERENNIAL

peace, peaceful
peach
peacock
peak
peal (of bells — see also peel)
peanut
pear (fruit — see also pair)
pearl
peasant
peat
pebble
peck
peculiar, peculiarity, peculiarities
pedal (on a cycle etc. — see also peddle)
peddle (sell on foot — see also pedal) pedlar
pedestrian
pedigree
peel (take off layer — see also peal)
peep
peer (look closely — see also pier)
peg
pellet
pelmet
pelt
pen
penalise
penalty, penalties, penalise
pence
pencil
pendant
pendulum
penetrate, penetration
penguin
penicillin
penknife, penknives
penniless
penny, pennies
pension, pensioner
people
pepper
peppermint
percent, percentage
perennial

PERFECT

perfect, perfection
perforate, perforating, perforation
perform, performance
perfume
perhaps
peril, perilous
perimeter
period, periodical
perish, perishable
permanent
permission, permissible
permit, permitted, permitting
perpetual
persecute, persecuting, persecution
persevere, perseverance
persist, persistent, persistence
person
personal, personally, personality, personalities
personnel
perspective
perspire, perspiring, perspiration
persuade, persuading, persuasion, persuasive
pessimist, pessimistic
pest, pester
pet, petted, petting
petal
petition
petrol
petticoat
petty, pettiness
pew
pewter
phantom
pheasant
phosphorous, phosphorescent, phosphorescence
photo, photograph, photos, photography, photocopy, photocopies
phrase
physical

PITIFUL

physics
physique
piano, pianist
pick, pickaxe
picket
pickle
picnic, picnicking
picture, picturesque, pictorial
pie
piece
pier (at seaside — see also peer)
pierce
pig, piggish
pigeon
pigmy
pigtail
pike
pile
pilfer
pill
pillar (column — see also pillow)
pillion
pillow (cushion — see also pillar)
pilot
pimple
pin, pinned, pinning
pinafore
pinch
pine
pineapple
pinion
pink
pint
pioneer
pip
pipe, piper, piping
pirate
pistol
piston
pit, pitted, pitting
pitch
pitchfork
pitfall
pitiful, pitiless

PITY

pity, pitied, pitying
pivot
placard
place (location — see also plaice) placing
plague
plaice (fish — see also place)
plain
plait
plan, planned, planning
plane, planing
planet
plank
plant
please, pleasing, pleasant, pleasure
plenty, plentiful
plot
plough
pluck
plug, plugged, plugging
plum
plumber
plumbline
plump
plunder
plunge, plunging
plural
plus
plush
ply
plywood
pneumatic
pneumonia
poach
pocket, pocketful
pod
poem
poetry, poet, poetic
point
poise
poison, poisonous
poke, poking
poker
polar
pole

POTTER

police
policy, policies
polio
polish
polite
politics, politician
poll
pollen
pollute, polluting, pollution
polo neck
polythene
pompous
pond
ponderous
pontoon
pony, ponies
pool
poor
pop
poplar
poppy, poppies
popular, popularity
populate, population
porcelain
pork
porous, pore
porridge or porage
port
portable
porter
portion
portrait
pose, posing
position
positive
possess, possessor, possession
possible, possibly, possibility
post, postage, postal
poster
post-mortem
postpone, postponement
postscript
potato, potatoes
potential, potentially
pothole, potholing
potter, pottery

POUCH / PROFICIENT

pouch
poultry
pounce, pouncing
pound
pour
poverty
powder
power, powerful
practical, practically
practice (*a* practice or *the* practice — see also practise)
practise (*to* practise — see also practice) practised, practising practises
prairie
praise, praising
pram
prance, prancing
prank
pray (request — see also prey) prayer
preach, preacher
precaution
precious
precipice
precise, precision
predict, prediction
prefabricated
prefect
prefer, preferring, preference
pregnant, pregnancy
prehistoric
prejudice
premature
premier
premises
premium
prepare, preparing, preparation
prescribe, prescription
presence
present, presents, presentation
presentable
preserve, preserving, preservation
president
press

prestige
presumably
presume
pretend, pretence
pretty, prettier, prettiest
prevent, prevention
previous
prey (victim — see also pray)
price, priceless
prick
prickle, prickly
pride
priest
primary
prime
primitive
prince
principal (most important, a person, etc. — see also principle)
principle (a rule — see also principal)
print
priority
prism
prison, prisoner
private, privacy
privet
privilege
prize, prize-giving
probable, probably
probation, probationary
probe
problem
procedure
proceed, proceeds
process, procession
prod
prodigy
produce, producing, production
producer
product
profession, professional
professor
proficient, proficiency

PROFILE

profile
profit, profitable
program (instruction to
  computer — see also
  programme)
programme (list of events
  — see also program)
progress, progressive
prohibit, prohibitive
project
projector
promenade, prom
prominent
promise
promote, promoting, promotion
prompt
prong
pronounce
pronunciation
proof
prop, propped, propping
propaganda
propel, propelled, propelling
propeller
proper
property
prophecy (*a* forecast —
  see also prophesy)
prophesy (*to* forecast — see
  also prophecy) prophesied,
  prophesying
prophet, prophetic
proportion, proportional,
  proportionately
propose, proposal, proposition
proprietor
prose
prosecute, prosecution
prospect, prospector
prosperous
protect, protection, protector,
  protective
protein
protest
protractor

PUSSY

proud
prove
proverb
provide, provision
province, provinces, provincial
provision, provisional
provoke, provoking
prowl
prune
psychology, psychologist
public
publication, publicity
publish
pudding
puddle
puff
pull
pulley, pulleys
pullover
pulp
pulpit
pulse
pulverise
pump
pun
punch
punctual
punctuate, punctuation
puncture, puncturing
punish, punishment
punt
puny
pup
pupil
puppet
puppy, puppies
purchase
pure, purely, purify
purple
purpose
purr
purse
pursue, pursuit
push
pussy, pussies

PUT

put, putting
putrid
putt
putty, puttied
puzzle, puzzled, puzzling
pyjamas
pylon
pyramid
python

Q

(See also words beginning
with c-)
quack
quadrangle
quaint
quake, quaking
qualify, qualified, qualifying
quality
quandary
quantity, quantities
quarantine
quarrel, quarrelled, quarrelling
quarrelsome
quarry, quarries
quart
quarter, quarterly
quartz
quay
queen
queer
quell
quench
query
question, questionnaire
queue, queueing
quick
quiet
quilt
quit
quite
quiver
quiz, quizzes

RANGER

quota
quote, quoting, quotation

R

(Words in brackets sound as though
they begin with r-)
rabbit
rabble
race, racing
racecourse
racial, racist, racism
rack
racket
radar
radiate, radiating, radiation
radiator
radio
radius, radii
raffle, raffling
raft
rafter
rag
rage, raging
ragged
raid, raider
rail, railing
railway
rain
rainbow, rainfall
raise, raising
raisin
rake, raking
rally, rallied, rallying
ram, rammed, ramming
ramble, rambling
ramp
ramshackle
ranch
rancid
random
rang
range, ranging
ranger

RANK

rank
ransack
ransom
(wrap, wrapped, wrapping)
rap, rapped, rapping
rapid, rapidity
rare
rarity, rarities
rascal
rash
rasher
rasp
raspberry, raspberries
rat
rate, rating
rather
ratio
ration
rattle, rattling
rattlesnake
rave, raving
ravenous
raw
ray
rayon
razor
reach
react, reaction
read
ready, readiness, readily
real, really
realise, realisation
realistic, realistically
reality
reappear, reappearance
rear
reason, reasonable
(wreath)
rebel, rebelled, rebelling, rebellious
rebellion
rebound
rebuild, rebuilt
recall
recapture

REGIMENT

receipt
receive, receiver
recent
reception, receptionist
receptive
recipe
recite, recitation, reciting
reckless
(wreck, wreckage)
reckon
recognise, recognition, recognising
recollect
recommend, recommendation
reconnaissance, reconnoitre
record
recorder
recover
recreation
recruit
rectangle, rectangular
red
redouble
reduce, reducing, reduction
reed
reef
reek
reel
re-enter
refer, referred, referring, referral
referee
reference
refine, refined
reflect, reflection
refresh, refreshment
refrigerator, refrigeration
refuel, refuelled, refuelling
refugee
refund
refuse, refusing, refusal
regard, regards
regardless
regent
regiment, regimental

REGION

region, regional
register, registration
regret, regretful, regrettable, regretting
regular, regularity
regulate, regulation, regulator
rehearse, rehearsal
reign (rule — see also rein)
rein (harness — see also reign)
reinforce, reinforcement
reject, rejection
rejoin
relate, relating, relation, relative
relax, relaxation
relay
release
relegate, relegation
reliable, reliability
relic
relief
relieve
religion, religious
reluctant, reluctance
rely, relied, relying, reliable
remain, remainder
remark, remarkable
remedy, remedied, remedies
remember, remembrance
remind, reminder
remote
remove, removing, removal (wrench)
rendezvous
renew, renewal
rent, rental
reopen
reorganise, reorganising, reorganisation
repaid
repair
repay
repeat
repeatedly
repetition

RETIRE

replace, replacement
reply, replied, replies
report, reporter
represent, representative
reprieve
reprimand
reprint
reproduce, reproduction
reptile
republic
repulsive
reputation
request
require, requiring
rescue, rescuing
research
resemble, resembling, resemblance
resent, resentful
reserve, reserving, reservation
reservoir
residence, resident
resign, resignation
resin
resist, resistance
resolution
resort
resource, resourceful
respect, respectability
respiration
respond
response, responsive
responsible, responsibility, responsibilities
rest, restful, restless
(wrestle, wrestling)
restaurant
restore, restoring, restoration
restrict, restriction
result
resume
retail
retain
retaliate, retaliation
retire, retirement

RETREAT

retreat
return
reunion
reveal
revenge
revenue
reverse, reversing, reversal
revert
revise
revolt, revolting
revolution, revolutionary
revolve
revolver
reward
rheumatism, rheumatic
rhinoceros
rhubarb
rhythm
rib, ribbed, ribbing
ribbon
rice
rich, richly, richness
riches
rick
rid
riddle, riddling
ride, riding
ridge
ridicule, ridiculous
rifle
rig, rigging
(wriggle, wriggling)
right
rigid
rim
rind
(wrinkle, wrinkling)
(wring = remove water — see also ring)
ring (a band, or peal of a bell — see also wring)
rink
rinse
riot
rip, ripped, ripping

ROYAL

ripe, ripen, ripeness
ripple, rippling
rise, rising, risen
risk, risky
(wrist)
(write, written, writing, wrote)
rival, rivalled, rivalling
river
rivet
road
roam
roar
roast
rob, robber, robbery, robberies
robin
robot
rock, rocky
rocket
rod
rode
rodent
rogue
roll
roller
romance, romantic
(wrong)
roof
rook
room, roomy
root
rope
rose
rot
rota
rotate, rotation, rotating
(wrote)
rough
round
roundabout
rouse
route
routine
row
royal, royalty

RUB

rub, rubbed, rubbing
rubber
rubbish
rubble
ruby, rubies
rudder
rude, rudeness
ruffian
ruffle, ruffling
rug
rugged
ruin
rule, ruling
ruler
rum
rumble, rumbling
rummage, rummaging
rumour
rump
rumple
run, running, runner
runaway
(wrung = removed water — see also rung)
rung (bell — see also wrung)
runway
rural
rush
rust, rusty
rustle
rut
ruthless
rye

S

sabotage
saccharin
sack
sacred
sacrifice, sacrificing
sad, sadder, sadly
saddle
safari

SAVOUR

safe
safeguard
sag
said
sail, sailor
saint
sake
salad
salary, salaries
sale
salesman
salon
saloon
salt
salute, saluting
salvage
same
sample, sampling
sanatorium
sand
sandal
sandpaper
sandwich
sane
sanitary
sanity
sank
sap
sapphire
sarcasm, sarcastic, sarcastically
sardine
sash
satchel
satellite
satin
satisfy, satisfaction, satisfactory
saturate
sauce, saucy
saucepan
saucer
sauna
sausage
savage, savagery
save, saving, saviour
savoury, savouries

SAW

saw, sawdust, sawn
say, saying, says
scaffold, scaffolding
scald
scale, scaling
scalp
scamper
scandal
scar
scarce, scarcity
scarcely
scare, scaring
scarecrow
scarf, scarves
scarlet
scatter, scatterbrain
scene, scenery, scenic
scent (odour — see also sent)
schedule
scheme, scheming
scholar, scholarship
school
science, scientific, scientifically
    scientist
scissors
scoff
scold
scoop
scorch
score, scoring, score-card
scorn, scornful
scour
scout
scramble, scrambling
scrap
scrap-book
scrape, scraping
scratch
scrawl
scream
screech
screen
screw
scribble, scribbling
scripture

SELF-CONTROL

scroll
scrub, scrubbed, scrubbing
scruff
scuffle, scuffling
scullery
sculptor, sculpture
scum
scurry, scurried
scuttle, scuttling
scythe, scything
sea, seaman, seaport, seashell,
    seaside, seaweed
seal
seam
search, searching
searchlight
season, seasoning
seat
secluded
second, secondly
secondary
second-hand
secrecy
secret
secretary, secretaries
sect
section
sector
secure, securing
sediment
see
seed, seedling
seek
seem
seen
seep
seesaw
seethe, seething
segment
seize, seizing
seldom
select
self, selves
self-conscious
self-control

SELF-DEFENCE

self-defence
selfish
self-service
sell
selvedge
semicircle, semicircular
senate, senator
send, sent
senior
sensation, sensational
sense, senseless
sensible, sensibly
sensitive
sent (told to go — see also scent)
sentence, sentencing
sentiment, sentimental
sentry, sentries
separate, separation, separating
septic
sequel
sequence
serenade, serenading
serene
serf
sergeant
serial
series
serious, seriousness
servant
serve, serving
service
serviette
session
set
settee
setting
settle, settling
settler, settlement
seven
seventeen
seventh
seventy
sever (cut — see also severe)
several

SHIELD

severe (strict — see also sever)
severity
sew (with needle and thread — see also sow) sewing machine
sewn
sewage, sewer
sex
shabby, shabbily
shack
shackle
shade, shady
shadow
shady, shadier, shadiest
shaft
shaggy
shake, shaken, shaking, shook
shallow
shame, shameful, shameless
shampoo
shamrock
shan't
shape, shapeless, shapely
share, sharing
shark
sharp, sharpen, sharpener
shatter
shave, shaving, shaven
shawl
sheaf, sheaves
shear, shears
sheath
shed
sheep
sheepish
sheer
sheet
sheik
shelf, shelves
shell
shelter
shelves, shelving
shepherd
sheriff
sherry
shield

SHIFT

shift
shin
shine, shining, shone
shiny
ship, shipping
shipwreck
shirk, shirker
shirt
shiver
shock, shocking
shoe
shone
shook
shoot
shop, shopping, shopkeeper
shore
short, shortage
shorthand
shortly
short-sighted
shot, shotgun
should, shouldn't
shout
shove, shoving
shovel, shovelled, shovelling
show, shown
shower, showery
shown
shrank
shrapnel
shriek
shrimp
shrink
shrivel, shrivelled
shrub, shrubbery
shrug, shrugged, shrugging
shrunk
shudder
shuffle, shuffling
shunt
shut
shute
shutter
shuttle
shuttlecock

SIT

shy
sick, sickness
side, sideboard
sideways
siding
siege
sieve, sieving
sift
sigh
sight
sign, signpost
signal, signalled, signalling
signature
signet
significance, significant
silence, silent
silhouette
silicon
silk
sill
silly, sillier, silliest
silo, silos
silt
silver
similar, similarity
simmer
simple, simply, simplicity
simplify
simulate, simulation
simultaneous
sin, sinful, sinning, sinned
since
sincere, sincerely
sinew
sing, sang, sung
singe, singeing
single
sinister
sink, sank, sunk
sip, sipped, sipping
siphon
sir
siren
sister, sister-in-law
sit, sat

SITUATED

situated, situation
six
sixteen
sixth
sixty
size
sizzle, sizzling
skate, skating
skeleton
sketch
skewer
ski, skiing, skis
skid, skidded, skidding
skies
skill, skilled
skim, skimmed, skimming
skimp, skimpy
skin, skinny
skin diving
skip, skipped, skipping
skipper
skirt
skulk
skunk
sky, skies
skylight, skyscraper
slab
slack, slacken
slam, slammed, slamming
slander
slang
slant, slanting
slap, slapped, slapping
slash
slate
slaughter
slave, slavery
slay, slain, slew
sledge
sleek
sleep, sleepless, sleepy, slept
sleeper
sleet
sleeve
slender

SNACK

slept
sleuth
slew
slice, slicing
slide, slid
slight, slightly
slim, slimmed, slimming
slime, slimy
sling
slip, slipped, slipping
slipper
slippery
slipshod
slit
slogan
slope, sloping
sloppy, sloppiness
slot
slouch
slow
slug, slugged, slugging
sluggish
slum
slump
slung
slush
sly
smack
small
smart
smash
smear
smell, smelt
smile, smiling
smith
smog
smoke, smoking, smoky
smooth
smother
smoulder
smudge, smudging
smug
smuggle, smuggling, smuggler
snack (a light meal — see also snake)

SNAG

snag
snail
snake (a reptile — see also snack)
snap, snapped, snapping
snapshot
snare, snaring
snarl
snatch
sneak
sneeze, sneezing
sniff
snip, snipped
snipe, sniping, sniper
snob, snobbish, snobbery
snore, snoring
snort
snout
snow, snowball, snowfall, snowflake
snub, snubbed, snubbing
snug
snuggle, snuggling
so
soak
soap
soar (fly high — see also sore)
sob, sobbed, sobbing
sober, sobered
social
society, societies
sock
socket
soda
sodden
sofa
soft, soften
soggy
soil
solar
sold
solder
soldier
sole, solely
solemn
solicitor

SPECIES

solid
solitary, solitude
solo, soloist, solos
soluble
solution
solve, solving
some, somehow, someone, somewhere, sometimes
son
son-in-law
sonic
soon
soot
soothe, soothing
soprano
sore (painful — see also soar)
sorrow
sorry
sort
sound
soup
sour
south, south-east, south-west
souvenir
sow (plant — see also sew)
soya, soya-bean
space, space-capsule, space-ship
spacious
spade
spaghetti
span, spanned, spanning
spaniel
spank
spanner
spare, sparing
spark, sparkle, sparkler
sparrow
spasm, spasmodic, spasmodically
spat
spatter
speak
spear
special, speciality
specialise, specialist
species

SPECIFIC	STANDARD
specific, specify	sprinkle, sprinkling
specimen	sprint
speck	sprout
spectacle, spectacular	sprung
spectrum	spun
speech, speechless	spur
speed	spurt
speedometer	spy, spied
speedway	squabble, squabbling
spell, spelling, spelt	squad
spend, spent	squadron
sphere	square
spice, spicy	squash
spider	squat, squatted, squatting
spill, spilt	squatter
spin, spinning, spin-dryer	squawk
spine, spinal	squeak
spindle	squeal
spinster	squeeze, squeezing
spiral, spiralled, spiralling	squint
spire	squirm
spirit	squirrel
spit, spat, spitting	squirt
spite, spiteful	stab, stabbed, stabbing
splash	stable
splendid	stack
splice, splicing	stadium
split, splitting	staff
splutter	stag
spoil, spoilt	stage, staging
spoke, spokesman	stagger
sponge	stain
sponsor	stair, staircase
spontaneous, spontaneously	stake (pointed post etc. — see also steak)
spoon, spoonful	stalactite
sport, sportsman	stalagmite
spot, spotted, spotting	stale
spotless	stalk
spotlight	stall
spout	stammer
sprain	stamp
sprawl	stampede
spray	stand, stand-by, standstill
spread	standard
spring, sprang, sprung	

STANDARDISE

standardise
staple
star, starry
starboard
starch
stare, staring
start
startle, startling
starve, starving, starvation
state, statement
statesman
static
station
stationary (still or stopped —
    see also stationery)
stationery (writing materials —
    see also stationary)
statistics
statue
status, status symbol
stay
steady
steak (meat — see also stake)
steal (take dishonestly — see
    also steel)
team
steel (metal — see also steal)
steep
steeple
steer
stem
stencil
step, stepped, stepping
sterile, sterilise
stern
stew
steward, stewardess
stick
sticky, stickiness
stiff
stile (step in a wall — see
    also style)
stiletto
still
stilts

STRENGTH

sting, stung
stink
stir, stirred, stirring
stirrup
stitched
stock
stockings
stoke, stoking, stoker
stole, stolen
stomach
stone
stood
stool
stoop
stop, stopped, stopping
stoppage
stopper
storage
store, storing
storeman
storey (floor of house — see
    also story) storeys
stork
storm
story (tale — see also storey)
    stories
stove
stowaway
straggle, straggling
straight, straightforward
strain
strand
strange
stranger
strangle
strap, strapped, strapping
straw
strawberry, strawberries
stray
streak
stream
streamer
streamlined
street
strength

57

STRETCH

stretch
stretcher
strict
stride, strode
strike, striking, struck
string
strip, stripped, stripping
stripe
strode
stroke, stroking
stroll
strong
struck
structure
struggle, struggling
strum, strummed, strumming
strung
stub, stubbed, stubbing
stubble
stubborn
stuck
stud
student
studio
study, studies
stuff
stuffing
stuffy
stumble, stumbling
stump
stun, stunned, stunning
stunt
stupid, stupidity
stutter
style, stylish
subject
submarine
submerge
submit, submission
substance
substantial
substitute
subtract, subtraction
suburb, suburban
subway

SUPREME

succeed
success, successful
such
suck
suction
sudden, suddenly
suds
suede
sufficient
suffocate, suffocating, suffocation
sugar
suggest, suggestion
suicide
suit
suitable
suite (a set, for example of furniture — see also sweet)
sulk, sulky
sulphur
sultana
sum
summary
summer
summit
summons
sun, sunny
sunburn, sunburnt
sung
sunk
sunlight
sunstroke
superhuman
superior, superiority
supermarket
supernatural
supersonic
superstition, superstitious
supervise, supervisor, supervision
supper
supply, supplies, supplied
support, supporter
suppose, supposing
supreme

SURE

sure, surely
surf
surface
surge
surgeon
surgery, surgical
surname
surplus
surprise, surprising
surrender
surround, surrounding
survey, surveyor
survive, survivor, surviving,
    survival
suspect, suspicion, suspicious
suspend
suspense
suspicion, suspicious
swallow
swam
swamp
swan
swarm
swat, swatted, swatting
sway
swear, swore, sworn
sweat
sweater, sweat-shirt
sweep, swept
sweet (not sour — see
    also suite)
sweetheart
swell, swelling, swollen
swept
swerve, swerving
swift
swim, swam, swum
swindle, swindler, swindling
swine
swing, swung
switch
swivel
swollen
swoop
sword

TARTAN

swore
sworn
swum
swung
syllable
sympathy, sympathise
synthetic
syringe
syrup
system, systematic

T

tab
table
tablespoon
tablet
tack
tackle, tackling
tact
tactics, tactical
tadpole
tag, tagged, tagging
tail
tailor
take, taking
talcum
tale
talent, talented
talk, talkative
tall
tame
tan, tanned, tanning
tangerine
tangle
tank
tanker
tap, tapped, tapping
tape, tape recorder
tar, tarred, tarring
target
tarnish
tart
tartan

TASK

task
taste, tasting
tattered
tattoo, tattooed, tattooing
taught (past of teach)
taut (tight)
tax, taxation
taxi, taxied, taxiing
tea
teach, teacher
team
tear, torn
tease, teasing
teaspoon, teaspoonful
technical
technique
teenager
tee-shirt
teeth
telegram
telephone, telephoning
teleprinter
telescope
television
tell, told
temper
temperament, temperamental
temperature
temple
temporary
tempt, temptation
ten, tenth
tenant
tend
tender
tennis
tense, tension
tent
tentacle
term
terminus
terrace
terrible, terribly
terrier
terrific, terrify, terror

THOUSAND

territory
test
testimonial
tether
text, textbook
textiles
texture
than
thank
that
thatched
thaw, thawed
theatre
theft
their (belonging to them — see also there)
them, themselves
then
theory, theories
there (in that place — see also their)
thermometer
thermos
thermostatic, thermostatically
these
they, they're, they'll
thick
thief, thieves
thigh
thimble
thin
thing
think
third
thirst, thirsty
thirteen
thirty
thorn
thorough
those
though
thought
thoughtful, thoughtfully, thoughtless
thousand

THRASH

thrash
thread
threat, threaten
three
threw (past of throw — see also through)
thrill
throat, throaty
throb, throbbed, throbbing
throne
throttle, throttling
through (across, along, from end to end —see also threw)
throw, thrown
thrust
thud, thudded, thudding
thumb
thump
thunder
tick
ticket
tickle, tickling
tide, tidal
tidy, tidier, tidiest
tie
tiger
tight
tile, tiling
till
tilt
timber
time, timing
timetable
timid
tin, tinplate, tinned, tinning, tinny
tingle, tingling
tinkle, tinkling
tint
tiny, tinier, tiniest
tip, tipped
tire, tiring
tissue
title

TOTAL

to
toad
toadstool
toast
tobacco
toboggan
today
toddle
toe
toffee
together
toilet
token
told
toll, tolled
tomato, tomatoes
tomb, tombstone
tomorrow
ton (English or U.S. weight — see also tonne)
tone, toning
tongue
tonic
tonight
tonne (metric weight — see also ton)
tonsils, tonsilitis
too
took
tool
tooth, toothache
top
topic
topple, toppling
torch
tore
torment
tornado, tornadoes
torpedo, torpedoes, torpedoed, torpedoing
tortoise
torture, torturing
toss
total

TOUCH

touch
tough, toughness
tour, tourist
tournament
tow
towards
towel, towelling
tower
town
toy
trace, tracing
track, track-suit
tractor
trade, trading
tradesman
trade union, trade unionist
traffic, trafficator
tragedy, tragedies, tragic
trail
trailer
train
traitor
tramp
trample, trampling
trampoline
tranquilizer
transfer, transferred,
    transferring
transform
transistor
translate, translation, translator
transmit, transmission,
    transmitter
transparent
transport
trap, trapped, trapping
trap-door
trash
travel, travelled, traveller
trawler
tray
treachery
tread
treason
treasure, treasurer, treasury

TRUNK

treat
treatment
treble, trebling
tree
tremble
tremendous
trench
trend
trespass, trespasser, trespassing
trestle
trial
triangle, triangular
tribe, tribal
trick
trickle, trickling
tried
trifle
trigger
trim, trimmed, trimming
trio
trip, tripper, tripping
triple
triplet
triumph, triumphant
trod, trodden
trolley
trombone
troop
trophy, trophies
tropical
trot, trotted, trotting
trouble, troubling,
    troublesome
trough
trousers
trousseau
trowel
truant, truancy
truce
truck
true, truly
trump
trumpet
truncheon
trunk

TRUST

trust, trustworthy
truth, truthful, truthfully
try, tried, tries
tub
tube, tubing, tubular
tuck
tuft
tug, tugged, tugging
tumble, tumbling
tumbler
tune, tuning
tunic
tunnel, tunnelled, tunnelling
turbine
turbo-jet
turf
turkey, turkeys
turn
turret
tusk
tutor
tweezers
twelve
twenty
twice
twig
twilight
twin
twine
twinkle
twist
two
tycoon
tying
type, typing, typewriter, typist
typical
tyre

U

ugly, uglier, ugliest
ulcer
ultimatum
umbrella

UPHILL

umpire
unanimous
uncanny
uncle
unconscious
uncouth
under
undercarriage
underground
undergrowth
underneath
understand, understanding, understood
undertaker
underwear
undress
unemployed, unemployment
uneven
unfasten, unfastened
unfit
unfortunate
unicorn
uniform
union
unique
unit
unite, unity
universal
universe
university
unless
unlimited
unlock
unnatural
unnecessary
unpleasant
unpopular, unpopularity
unravel, unravelled, unravelling
unscrupulous
untie, untying, untied
until
untruth
unusual
unwell
uphill

63

UPON

upon
upper
upright
uproar
upset, upsetting
upside-down
upstairs
up-to-date
upwards
urge, urging
urgent
use, useful, useless
usherette
usual, usually
utensil
utility
utmost

V

vacancy, vacancies
vacant
vacation
vaccinate, vaccinating, vaccination
vacuum
vague
vain
valentine
valet
valid
valley, valleys
value, valuable
valve
van
vandal, vandalise, vandalism
vanish
vapour, vaporised
varied, variety, varieties
various
varnish
vary, varied, varies, varying
vase
vast

VIRTUAL

vault
vegetable
vehicle
veil
vein
velocity
velvet
vending-machine
veneer
vengeance
venom, venomous
ventilate, ventilation
ventriloquist
venture
verdict
verge, verging
vermin, verminous
versatile
verse
version
vertical, vertically
very
vessel
vest
vet, veterinary surgeon
veteran
veto, vetoed
viaduct
vibrate, vibration, vibrating
vicar, vicarage
vice
vicious
victim
victory, victories, victorious
video-cassette, videotape
view, viewpoint
villa
village
villain, villainous
vinegar
vineyard
violent, violence
violet
violin, violinist
virtual, virtually

VIRUS

virus
visible, visibility
vision
visit, visitor
visual, visualise, visual-aids
vital
vitamin
vivid
vixen
vocabulary
vocal
voice
volcano
volley, volleyball
volt, voltage
volume
voluntary
volunteer
vomit
vote, voting
voucher
vowel
voyage
vulgar, vulgarity
vulture

W

wad
waddle, waddling
wade, wading
wafer
wag, wagged, wagging
wages, wage-packet
wagon
wail
waist, waistcoat
wait
waiter, waitress
wake, waking, waken
walk
wall
wallet
walnut

WELCOME

wander
want
war
ward
warden
warder, wardress
wardrobe
warehouse
warfare
warm, warmth
warn, warning
warplane
warrant
wary, warily
was, wasn't
wash, washing
washer
wasp
waste, wasting, wasteful
watch
watchful
watchman
water, waterfall
waterproof
watertight
wave, waving, wavy
wax
way, wayside
weak
wealth, wealthy
weapon
wear
weary, wearily, weariness
weasel
weather (rain, snow etc. — see also whether)
weave, weaving, woven
web, webbed
wedding
wedge, wedging
weed
week, weekend, weekly
weigh, weight
weird
welcome

WELD

weld
welfare
well
wellingtons
went
wept
were
west
wet
whack
whale
what, whatever
wheat
wheel, wheelbarrow
wheeze, wheezing, wheezy
when
where, whereabouts
whether
which
while, whilst
whine, whining
whip, whipped, whipping
whirlwind
whiskers
whisky
whisper
whistle, whistling
white
whiz
who, who's (= who is)
whole, wholly
whom
whooping cough
whose (belonging to)
why
wick
wicked, wickedness
wicker
wicket
wide, width
widow, widower
wife, wives
wig
wild, wildness
will, will-power

WORRY

willing
wily
win, winning, winner
wince, wincing
winch
wind
windcheater
windfall
windmill
window
windscreen
wine
wing, winged
wink
winter, wintry
wipe, wiping
wire, wiring
wireless
wisdom
wise
wish
wit, witty
witch, witchcraft
with
within
without
witness
wives
wizard
wobble, wobbling
wolf, wolves
woman, women
wonder, wonderful
won't
wood, wooden
woodpecker
woodwork
wool, woolly, woollen
word
wore
work
world
worm
worn
worry, worried

WORSE

worse, worst
worth, worthless
would, wouldn't
wound
wrap, wrapped, wrapping
wreath
wreck, wreckage
wrench
wrestle, wrestling
wriggle, wriggling
wrinkle, wrinkling
wring, wrung
wrist
write, writing, written, wrote
wrong
wrote
wrung

X

Xmas
X-ray

ZOOM

Y

yard
yawn
year, yearly
yeast
yell
yellow
yes
yesterday
yet
yolk
you, you'd, you're, you've
young, youngster
your, yours
you're (you are)
yourself, yourselves
youth

Z

zebra
zero
zigzag
zip, zipper
zone
zoo
zoom

Names

Girls

Afzhal	Charlotte	Habib
Alison	Christine	Hazel
Amanda	Claire, Clare	Helen
Angela	Deborah, Debra	Hilary
Ann, Anne	Diana	Jacqueline
Anuradha	Diane	Jane
Asha	Eileen	Janet
Beverley	Elizabeth	Jean
Bridget	Emma	Jennifer
Carol, Carole	Frances	Jill
Caroline	Gillian	Joan
Catherine	Gwen	Joanna, Joanne

Josephine	Margaret	Sandra
Judith	Maria	Sara, Sarah
Julia, Julie	Marian, Marion	Sheila
Kamala	Mary	Sita
Karen	Nalini	Soma
Kathleen	Nicola	Sudha
Laila	Patricia	Susan, Sue
Lakshmi	Paula	Teresa
Lesley	Raziya	Tracey, Tracy
Lila	Rebecca	Uma
Linda	Rosemary	Valerie
Lindsay	Roshni	Victoria, Vicky
Louise	Ruth	Wendy
Lucy	Sally	

Boys

	Gary, Garry	Michael
	Geoffrey	Neil
Adrian	Gerald	Nicholas
Ahmed	Giles	Nigel
Alan, Allan	Glen, Glenn	Noel
Alastair	Gopal	Owen
Alexander	Govind	Patrick
Ali	Graham, Grahame	Paul
Andrew	Guy	Peter
Anil	Hari	Philip
Anthony	Howard	Rama
Ashok	Hugh	Raymond
Barry	Ian	Richard
Benjamin	James	Robert
Brian	Jason	Roger
Charles	Jayant	Salim
Christopher	John	Simon
Clive	Jonathan	Stephen, Steven
Colin	Joseph	Stewart, Stuart
Daniel	Keith	Sudhir
David	Kenneth	Suresh
Dean	Kevin	Terence
Derek, Derrick	Krishna	Thomas
Duncan	Leslie	Timothy
Edward	Malcolm	Trevor
Evan	Mark	Vincent
Francis	Martin	William
Gareth	Matthew	Zia

Days of the Week

Sunday
Monday
Tuesday
Wednesday
Thursday
Friday
Saturday

Months

January
February
March
April
May
June
July
August
September
October
November
December

Holidays, etc.

New Year's Day
Easter
May Day
Whitsun
Spring Bank Holiday
August Bank Holiday
Hallowe'en
Christmas
Boxing Day
Dassara
Diwali
Bakr-Id
Holi
Pongal
Ganesh-Chaturti

The Seasons

Spring
Summer
Autumn
Winter

Places

Africa
America
Antarctica
Arctic
Argentina
Asia
Australia
Austria
Bahamas
Bangladesh
Barbados
Belgium
Bermuda
Brazil
Britain
Bulgaria
Canada
Chile
China
Czechoslovakia
Denmark
Egypt
England
Europe
Finland
France
Germany
Ghana
Gibraltar
Greece
Grenada
Hawaii
Holland
Hong Kong
India
Ireland
Israel
Italy
Jamaica
Japan
Kenya
Libya
Luxemburg
Malaysia
Malta
Mexico
Morocco
Netherlands

New Zealand
Nigeria
Norway
Pakistan
Peru
Poland
Portugal
Romania
Russia

Scotland
Singapore
South Africa
Spain
Sri Lanka
Sweden
Switzerland
Tanzania
Trinidad & Tobago

Turkey
Uganda
United States
Vietnam
Yugoslavia
Wales
Zaire
Zambia
Zimbabwe

PERSONAL SPELLING LIST
MAKE A NOTE OF SPELLINGS NEEDED WHICH ARE NOT IN 'SPELL IT'

A

PERSONAL SPELLING LIST
MAKE A NOTE OF SPECIFIC WORDS NEEDED WHICH ARE NOT YET SPELLED.

B

C

D

E

F

G

H

I	J

K	L

M

N

O

P	Q

R

S

T

U	V

W	X

Y	Z